OLD

GLORY

OLD GLORY

Nancy S. Grant

CRESCENT BOOKS

NEW YORK / AVENEL, NEW JERSEY

This 1992 edition published by CRESCENT BOOKS
distributed by Outlet Book Company, Inc.,
a Random House Company,
40 Engelhard Avenue, Avenel, New Jersey 07001

ISBN 0-517-06986-5

Printed and bound in Hong Kong

The Image Bank
111 Fifth Avenue, New York, NY 10003

Writer: Nancy S. Grant
Designer: Ann-Louise Lipman
Editor: Sara Colacurto
Production: Valerie Zars
Photo Researcher: Edward Douglas
Assistant Photo Researcher: Robert V. Hale
Editorial Assistant: Carol Raguso

Table of Contents

Do you remember the first time you *really* saw the American flag and felt that delicious surge of recognition that comes with understanding? Did you stand just a little taller—with a heart-swelling rush of pride—at the annual Fourth of July parade? Did you share the hot flush of excitement as an Olympic athlete stood up on the block to accept a hard-won gold medal? Or did you lean forward to the edge of your seat in a dimly lit movie theater as your favorite screen hero marched forward into battle against terrible odds?

Or perhaps you weren't a spectator at all, but involved in the action. Remember standing in front of your grade school classmates that cold Tuesday morning to lead the Pledge of Allegiance? Marching in the color guard before the Homecoming football game? Struggling to hold the perfect salute under the hawklike eye of the Drill Sergeant at boot camp?

Or did you see Old Glory (before you even knew the nickname) from afar, the symbol of a foreign nation quite unlike your homeland, yet beckoning to you across the miles with its stars and stripes symbolizing freedom?

A NEW CONSTELLATION

That marvelous concoction of red, white, and blue, elegant in its simplicity, brings forth a host of memories each time we look at it. But though the present arrangement of its gleaming stars and broad stripes is as familiar and welcome to us as the smiles of our families and friends, the men and women who forged one nation out

of chaos struggled under a different banner—actually, many banners.

As the earliest rough frontier outposts of the Spanish, Dutch, British, and French empires grew into thriving colonies, competition among the Old World powers heated up in the struggle for prized raw materials and geographic advantage. European flags were hoisted up—and down—all over the vast North American continent during a series of squabbles, skirmishes, and full-scale wars.

Despite such distractions, commerce flourished and colonists stitched together their own distinctive flags to identify merchant ships. New York ships sported white banners with black beavers to indicate the prospering fur trade, while Massachusetts Bay and other New England ships sailed under a pine tree ensign.

Throughout the long French and Indian Wars (1689 to 1763), the English colonists welcomed two British flags, the Union Flag of the Royal Navy and the Meteor Flag of the English land forces, as symbols of much-needed money, arms, and manpower. But by 1775, those two flags were just as likely to inspire anger, even outright disgust. The colonists, emboldened by their prosperity and savoring their successes in coping with the unique problems that arose so far from the "motherland," resented the Crown's constant meddling and outrageous demands.

Searching for a quick and easy way to publicize their growing dissatisfaction, they turned their flags into billboards. They embroidered slogans such as "Liberty or Death" and "Don't Tread on Me" on their rattlesnake flags, and even added protest messages to British flags.

One of the earliest such flags was raised in Taunton, Massachusetts: A replica of the British Red Ensign, its solid red field sported bold white letters proclaiming "Liberty and Union." Other popular slogans of the time were "Hope" and "An Appeal to Heaven."

Yet King George and his Parliament continued to misunderstand the depth of feeling and purpose behind the petitions and protests that the colonists mustered after each fresh British blunder. Finally, when the British Army marched on Concord on April 19, 1775, there was no mistaking the colonists' intentions:

> *"By the rude bridge that arched the flood,*
> *Their flag to April's breeze unfurled,*
> *Here the embattled farmers stood,*
> *And fired the shot heard round the world."*

That's how American poet Ralph Waldo Emerson imagined the scene years later; we must use our imaginations to fill in the details. We simply don't know what that first American battle flag looked like, although many historians suggest the Three County Troop banner as the most likely candidate. A local flag dating back to 1659, it featured an arm holding a dagger.

As fighting broke out up and down the Atlantic coast, patriots rallied behind all sorts of local flags and invented new combinations on the spur of the moment. Even the so-called "Bunker Hill Flag" was nothing more than the British blue ensign with the addition of a green pine tree on the St. George's Cross. A brave gesture, to be sure, and inspiring to the locals who knew the story, yet such flags presented a terrible problem in the swirl of battle: they could all too easily be mistaken for the enemy's. Then too, the variety of flag designs did little to unify the ragtag assortment of militias going up against the British colossus.

As 1775 drew to a close, someone—no one knows exactly who or where—created the first truly "national" flag, one that could fly over all the colonies without giving any individual section preference. The Continental Colors, or Grand Union Flag, featured a canton (the square in the upper corner) bearing the English crosses of St. George and St. Andrew—but the field, extending lengthwise across the banner, consisted of 13 alternating red and white stripes symbolizing each of the colonies. While the continued use of British symbols conveyed their hope of eventual reconciliation with the Mother Country, the distinctive and original design of the field recognized the colonies' growing sense of unity.

Commander-in-Chief George Washington liked the design so much that he chose it to be flown to celebrate the formation of the Continental Army on New Years' Day, 1776. The Grand Union Flag was proudly raised on Prospect Hill in Somerville, near his headquarters at Cambridge, Massachusetts, that very morning.

It was widely accepted and proudly flown (though never officially required, and often simply in addition to the local flag) from one end of the Eastern Seaboard to the other for another six months until the Continental Congress declared Independence in July 1776. That momentous event, accompanied by plenty of toasts and bell-ringing, meant that a flag incorporating British symbols clearly wouldn't do.

But the delegates were far too busy trying to figure out how to back up their brave words with suitable actions to worry about designating an appropriate new flag. For the time being, choosing a battle standard remained a matter of individual taste for each fighting unit on land and at sea. Almost a full year passed before Congress got around to saying something official about the subject.

Finally, on June 14, 1777, Congress resolved "That the flag of the thirteen United States be thirteen stripes, alternate red and white; that the union be thirteen stars, white in a blue field, representing a new constellation." And that's *all* they said—no mention of how many points the stars should have or a layout of just how they should be arranged to form this "new constellation."

Instead, we have the charming story of Betsy Ross, the Philadelphia seamstress. According to tradition, General George Washington, Robert Morris, and Colonel George Ross paid a call on Colonel Ross's nephew's widow and showed Betsy a drawing of a flag with six-pointed stars. She suggested five-pointed stars, arranged in a circle, and obligingly sewed up a prototype.

It's a great story, often embellished with quotes from the participants—the only trouble is, the story wasn't made public until 1870, when Mrs. Ross's grandson, William J. Canby, read a paper to the Historical Society of Pennsylvania recounting a childhood conversation he had with her when she was 84 years old. No sketch has yet been found, and historians have searched in vain through old newspapers, as well as delegates' notes and diaries, for clues as to what exactly they had in mind that morning, anything to substantiate the details. They can't prove it—and they can't disprove it—so the legend continues to delight us.

THE STRUGGLE FOR RECOGNITION

No matter who created the first Stars and Stripes (other unprovable stories involve American naval hero John Paul Jones, Declaration of Independence signer Francis Hopkinson, and Long Islander John Hulbert), our flag—and our national resolve—immediately faced severe tests.

One of the first known appearances of the "new constellation" was during the Battle of Bennington in

1777. In mid-August, a detachment of British Major General Burgoyne's forces, a group of Hessian dragoons under command of Lieutenant Colonel Friedrich Baum, crossed paths with patriot General John Stark's troops along the Walloomsac River in Vermont. On the afternoon of August 16, 1777, the 49-year-old patriot general turned to his troops and said, "My men, yonder are the Hessians. They were bought for seven pounds and ten pence a man. Are you worth more? Prove it. Tonight, the American flag floats from yonder hill or Molly Stark sleeps a widow!"

Prove it they did. Molly kissed her husband yet again, and the flag his soldiers so valiantly carried to the top of the hill can still be seen today, lovingly preserved at the Bennington Museum. The Bennington battle flag's constellation of stars is arranged so that two stars enliven the upper corners of the blue canton, the remaining eleven stars form a semi-circle over the legend "76" (even though Congress never said anything about adding a date), and the field's red and white stripes are in reversed order—yet it's unmistakably a true American flag.

The Revolutionary War was fought as much at sea as on land, and naval triumphs soon followed. The Stars and Stripes, fluttering above John Paul Jones's ship the *Ranger*, was first honored by a foreign nation in February 1778 when the French Royal Navy exchanged salutes with the *Ranger*, their respective guns booming 13 times each. On April 24th the same year, the *Ranger* defeated the British ship *Drake*, forcing its crew to strike their colors; the Stars and Stripes was then hoisted in victory.

In battle after battle, many versions of our national ensign (often with the stripes arranged vertically) emerged triumphant until at last British commander General Cornwallis surrendered to General George Washington on October 18, 1791, at Yorktown. With suitably decorous military ceremony, the British flag came down, and the Stars and Stripes went up—and the salutes and cheering thundered through the air.

Throughout the spring and summer, victorious patriots—and their handmade versions of the new American flag—gradually returned to areas once held by the British, and a peace treaty was finally signed on September 3. Evacuation Day for New York, the last British garrison and Loyalist stronghold, was set for November 25. According to a meticulously designed plan, British troops would withdraw section by section, to be followed by a symbolic parade of dignitaries and American soldiers, even General Washington himself. Tensions were still running high as the ceremony got under way and the American flag inadvertently provided comic relief.

A certain Mrs. Day, proprietress of Day's Tavern on Murray Street, eager to have her American flag on display for the advancing American parade, raised the Stars and Stripes *before* the appointed time. When an over-zealous British provost marshall still in the neighborhood demanded that she lower it, she took up her broom and proceeded to thrash him. To the delight of the crowd clapping and cheering in the street, his wig slid down, her flag stayed up—and wags began calling it the last "battle" of the American Revolution.

Later that afternoon, when the last of the British guards had withdrawn to their waiting ships in the harbor, a company of American artillery and one of light infantry marched down Broadway to take possession of Fort George. But this time the joke was on the Americans: Earlier that morning, when the British occupants had run their flag up the staff for the last time, they didn't do it the usual way—they *nailed* it in place, removed the ropes and rigging, and then slathered the entire pole with grease.

Three times the Americans attempted to shinny up the pole to set things right—and three times they slid right back down to the bottom, all under the watchful eyes of the assembled dignitaries. Finally, a resourceful sailor ascended the pole driving nails for footholds and attaching cleats as he went aloft, trailing a fresh rope tied to his waist. At last he reached the top, yanked down the foreign flag, attached the new halyard to the pulley, then went back down the way he'd come. While the British and Hessian troops watched from the harbor, an artillery officer hoisted the Stars and Stripes to its rightful place, and the American guns boomed out a joyful salute.

WHAT SO PROUDLY WE HAIL

By 1814, it was quite a different flag that waved triumphantly over another American fort. Shortly after the Revolutionary War, Kentucky and Vermont were added to the list of United States. The two new states insisted on equal status with the original states, and that included representation on the flag.

"Change the flag!" gasped the senators and representatives. "A consummate piece of frivolity!" huffed one. "Trifling!" sniffed another. "It would cost too much to replace our old ones!" chimed in another.

But on January 8, 1794, Congress (by a vote of 50 to 42) decreed: "Be it enacted, that from and after the first day of May, anno domini 1795, the flag of the United States be fifteen stripes, alternate red and white. That the Union be fifteen stars, white in a blue field."

It was under this newest constellation that Congress and the rest of the federal government moved to their permanent quarters in the fledgling city of Washington, D.C., the Louisiana Purchase doubled the nation's land area, and Lewis and Clark completed their overland exploration to the Pacific shores and back again. The future looked bright for the United States—until war broke out in 1812 over Britain's attempts to regulate American shipping and other activities while Britain was at war with France.

By August 1814, British troops had set fire to the new American Capitol and the White House (President Madison and his cabinet had already fled to a safer location), then sailed off for Baltimore intent on wreaking more havoc.

On September 6 the citizens of Baltimore asked young lawyer Francis Scott Key and his friend John S. Skinner to row out to the British flagship in the harbor to negotiate the release of Dr. Beanes, whom the British were threatening to hang. Although Key accomplished his mission, the British Vice-Admiral wouldn't let the Americans return to shore immediately for fear they'd reveal details of his plan to bombard Fort McHenry. The three men were transferred to another ship to wait.

In the meantime, while Maryland's defenders met British land challenges, Fort McHenry commander Major Armistead prepared for the anticipated assault as best he could. Discovering that the fort had no flag, he asked Mary Young Pickersgill to make one. Assisted by her mother and her daughter (some say her helpers were her two nieces), she completed a huge 30-by-42-foot flag in time for it to be raised before the long-awaited bombardment began.

At six in the morning on September 13, the British ships began hurling bombs at the fort. All day and all night, for 25 hours, explosions rent the air—and when the racket finally stopped on the 14th, Key and his companions, far out in the harbor, waited for enough light to reveal what might be left of the fort. Peering through their glasses, they saw the American flag stirring in the morning's breeze above the fort, and in a flash of inspiration Key captured the moment in an exuberant poem:

Oh, say, can you see, by the dawn's early light,
What so proudly we hailed at the twilight's last
 gleaming?
Whose broad stripes and bright stars through the
 perilous fight,
O'er the ramparts we watched, were so gallantly
 streaming?
And the rockets' red glare, the bombs bursting in air,
Gave proof through the night that our flag was still
 there.
Oh, say, does that star-spangled banner yet wave
O'er the land of the free and the home of the brave?

Printed under the title "The Defense of Fort McHenry," and with the notation to sing it to the tune of "Anacreon in Heaven," a popular song of the time, people soon began referring to it as "that Star-Spangled Banner song." Immediately popular, it remained just one of several favorite patriotic airs until it was finally adopted as our national anthem on March 3, 1931; it's the only national anthem in the world devoted to a flag.

OLD GLORY AND THE ORDEALS OF BATTLE

Star-spangled though it was, the banner Key immortalized wasn't strictly accurate—Tennessee (1796), Ohio (1803), and Louisiana (1812) had already been admitted to the Union. Indiana followed in 1816; by 1817 Mississippi was poised to become the twentieth state. If Congress continued the precedent set with the admission of Kentucky and Vermont, those broad stripes would soon begin to look like ribbons, getting thinner and thinner with the addition of each new state. Captain Samuel Reid, a naval hero of the War of 1812, and New York Congressman Peter Wendover recommended a compromise: Return to the original thirteen stripes (suitably broad) and let the stars alone represent the total number of states.

On March 25, 1818, a bill entitled "An Act to Establish the Flag of the United States" passed in the House, providing that "from and after the fourth of July next, the flag of the United States be thirteen horizontal stripes, alternate red and white; that the union have twenty stars, white in a blue field." Anticipating the future, the bill's second section further stated "that on the admission of every new State into the Union, one star be added to the union of the flag; and that such addition shall take effect on the fourth of July next succeeding each admission." The Senate passed the bill unanimously, President Madison signed it into law on April 4, and the nation had its first permanent flag law.

After the Mexican War established the right to fly the American flag from Oregon to Texas, the number of stars spangling that banner grew steadily. Despite the endless wrangling over slavery and states' rights which slowed down the admission process, the flags at Lincoln's inauguration on March 4, 1861, sported 33 stars. But seven of the states represented there claimed their stars belonged elsewhere—on the new flag adopted by the Confederate States of America that same day.

Like their Revolutionary forefathers, whom they admired and identified with, the secessionists incorporated the same elements of their "mother" country's flag in their new national banner. Its blue canton featured a circle of seven stars, and the field was red and white. But instead of seven corresponding stripes, it had three wide bands, red at the top, white for the center, then a long bar of red all across the bottom, hence the nickname the "Stars and

Bars." They learned all over again the hard way why such borrowing wasn't practical—under battle conditions it was often too difficult to decipher which flag was which.

But there was no mistaking the identity of the troops under what became known as the "Battle Flag of the Confederacy." Usually square rather than oblong, its solid field was criss-crossed with two diagonal blue stripes set with 13 white stars—a bit of wishful thinking since even though Kentucky and Missouri had plenty of Rebel sympathizers, both states remained officially neutral and never joined the eleven who had fled the Union.

It was yet another Confederate flag that finally provided a rallying point for Rebel troops—and like the Union's flag, it too was the subject of a song. Harry McCarthy's verses set out the Rebel cause and the stirring refrain, "Hurray! Hurrah! for Southern Rights hurrah! Hurrah for the Bonnie Blue Flag that bears a single star," immediately inspired civilians and troops throughout the Cotton Belt. That particular flag—and the song— became so important to the Southern cause that when Federal troops occupied New Orleans in 1862, General Benjamin "The Beast" Butler imposed a $25 fine for anyone caught singing, playing, or even so much as whistling "The Bonnie Blue Flag."

While some fiery-eyed Rebels insisted that the Union's flag should be redesigned to reflect the loss of states, as the war progressed it actually *gained* stars. The 34th star, for Kansas, took its place among the others on July 4, 1861. Then on July 4, 1863, the 35th star was added for West Virginia: Disagreeing with secession, Union sympathizers in Virginia's far western counties organized their own government, becoming the only state carved out of an existing one without the larger body's consent.

Deep in Rebel territory, possession of *any* Union flag—never mind how many stars—meant danger. While the Confederate flag flew over Tennessee's capital in Nashville, Rebel forces made life miserable for Union sympathizers, especially Captain William Driver. Retired from his exploits aboard the brig *Charles Doggett* since 1837, he'd brought along a treasured flag from his days at sea. Depending on who's telling the story, it was either on the occasion of his twenty-first birthday or just before he set sail as master of his first ship that he saw the flag waving in the breeze across Salem's harbor and exclaimed, "It's the most glorious flag I ever saw, Mother! I'll call her 'Old Glory!'"

The nickname might have remained known only to sailors, but by the time the Civil War erupted, everyone in and around Nashville recognized Captain Driver's "Old Glory." The Rebels were determined to destroy it, but repeated searches revealed no trace of the hated banner.

Then on February 25, 1862, Union forces captured Nashville and raised the American flag over the capital. It was a rather small ensign and immediately folks began asking Captain Driver if "Old Glory" still existed. Accompanied by welcome soldiers this time, Captain Driver went back to his home, and began ripping at the seams of his bedcover. As the stitches holding the quilt-top to the batting unraveled, the onlookers peered inside—and saw the 24-starred original "Old Glory" safely intact where it had been hidden during the desperate days and nights of war.

Captain Driver gently gathered up the flag and returned with the soldiers to the capital. Though he was sixty years old, the Captain climbed up to the dome to replace the smaller banner with his beloved flag. The Sixth Ohio Regiment cheered and saluted—and later adopted the nickname "Old Glory" as their own, telling and re-telling the story of Captain Driver's devotion to the flag we honor yet today.

FROM FLAG DAY TO EVERYDAY

Emerging victorious from the cataclysm of civil war trailing three nicknames, a rousing patriotic song, and a much-lengthened roll-call of heroes, the American flag had won a secure place in the memories of the American people. But it still wasn't the commonplace object that has become such a familiar part of our everyday lives. That transformation took place largely because of the expansion of mass production and new forms of mass communications—and the tireless efforts of a few dedicated individuals.

When Americans gathered to celebrate the nation's Centennial on July 4, 1877, crowds surged under and near treasured flags—but they were merely a backdrop for prayers, fireworks, and speeches that focused not on past glories but on hopes for an exciting future. That summer's most exuberant episode of flag-waving came later, when the citizens of Colorado (the "Centennial State") celebrated their admission into the Union; as residents of the newly minted 38th state, parading with the Star-Spangled Banner was a delightful new privilege. The following summer, on the flag's 100th birthday, Congress ordered that the flag be flown over public buildings on June 14th. But it was a one-time gesture that wasn't repeated until the twentieth century.

Instead, the idea for regular observances of Flag Day originated at the grass-roots level. George Bolch, a New York City kindergarten principal, held patriotic exercises at his school on June 14, 1889, and soon the state legislature passed a law requesting such observances in schools throughout the state. Meanwhile, Pennsylvanian

William T. Kerr urged similar programs in his state, and Bernard J. Cigrand persuaded his fellow Chicagoans, who founded the American Flag-Day Association in 1894, to stick with the flag's actual birthdate for their celebrations instead of moving them to the third Saturday in June. Another Pennsylvanian, Joseph H. Hart, led the campaign in his city that culminated in the formation of the Allentown Flag Day Association in 1907.

National groups such as the Fraternal Order of Elks and the American Legion were busy, too, encouraging Flag Day activities in their communities throughout the country. Finally, in 1916, President Woodrow Wilson issued a national proclamation on behalf of a Flag Day that year, and in 1927 President Calvin Coolidge followed suit. But it wasn't until 1949 that President Truman officially designated June 14 as Flag Day.

Establishing a national day of honor for Old Glory was certainly a slow process, and it might never have happened at all except for the fact that commercially manufactured flags had become readily available. From the earliest days of the Republic, flags had been hand-sewn out of everything from women's petticoats and dress materials to bits of prisoners' uniforms and blanket scraps in Libby Prison during the Civil War. The preferred material, of course, was bunting, a particular style of light cotton or woolen cloth, commonly manufactured abroad and sold off the bolt here. Then in the later half of the nineteenth century, high tariffs on imported fabrics combined with American mechanical ingenuity to launch a new domestic industry, commercial flag-making.

Gradually flags made of American materials and by American workers began appearing in communities from the Atlantic to the Pacific; by some estimates as many as 30,000 were put into use in school buildings alone. Those schools served not just the sons and daughters of American veterans but also the children of increasingly large waves of immigrants. And as the flag moved into civilian life, a new problem developed—how to instill and preserve respect for what was still essentially an emblem of military might and national power. Marching about "playing soldier" was one thing, but the flag clearly wasn't a toy.

In 1892, a children's weekly magazine, *The Youth's Companion*, published a brief sentence for youngsters to recite as part of the celebrations commemorating the 400th anniversary of Columbus's landing in the New World. Francis Bellamy, probably inspired and assisted by co-worker James B. Upham, wrote out a simple affirmation that he hoped would endure beyond this one special occasion: "I pledge allegiance to my Flag and the Republic for which it stands—one nation indivisible—with liberty and justice for all." That concise declaration (with the phrase "the flag of the United States of America" substituted for clarity in 1923, and the assertion that it stands for one nation "under God" added in 1954) has introduced generations of Americans to the duties and responsibilities of citizenship in a country still striving to live up to the promise.

And though the Pledge of Allegiance promptly became a standard feature of school days, adult club meetings, and the like, the flag itself was anything but standard. Even as late as 1912, there was still tremendous variety among the banners being saluted. The stars might be arranged in staggered rows, or concentric circles, sometimes with a larger star in the center; even the entire canton often varied in size. When New Mexico and Arizona finally met the requirements for admission as states that year, thus filling in the last blank spaces on the continental map of the United States, the government took advantage of the opportunity to regularize certain aspects of the flag.

Using the hoist (height) of the flag as one unit, each of the other dimensions was expressed in proportion to it, such as setting the fly (length) at 1.9 units, and the diameter of each star at 0.0616. But the exact placement of the stars became, as it still is, a presidential prerogative. Accepting the recommendations of a joint military committee headed by Admiral Dewey, President William Howard Taft ordered that the 48 stars of the 25th American flag be arranged in six rows of eight stars. Besides regulating the internal proportions of flags, legislation and executive orders also set out standard overall sizes for manufacturers to follow when making flags for specific government uses.

As the flag moved from being strictly a military emblem or political symbol into the mainstream of American life, appearing in everything from vaudeville skits to baseball games, marking the beginning of Independence Day parades and the grand openings of department stores, it took on a new aura—that of a living thing. Oh, the grouches scoffed and sneered at giving a mere piece of cloth such honor, but that was just the point: With so many banners hanging all over the place, the newest danger to the flag was that it would become *too* common.

Each branch of the armed services, as well as the diplomatic corps, followed certain customs regarding the use of the flag, but few civilians were aware of all the "do's" and "don'ts." So in 1923, under the auspices of the American Legion, representatives of more than five dozen organizations met in Washington D.C. on Flag Day to devise a code of etiquette to guide ordinary people. The Flag Code's 15 sections specify instructions and examples of when, where, and how to display the American flag, either alone or as a part of a group; 17 further cautions include the most widely known rule:

"Do not let the Flag touch the ground or the floor, or trail in the water."

Members of the American Legion, other patriotic organizations, and individuals spend countless hours teaching the rules to each new generation of Americans, stressing, as the Code itself points out, "that the Flag represents the living country and is itself considered as a living thing." The flag is often compared to a dear friend, due every kindness and genuine respect.

FRESH HOPES AND NEW GLORIES

Analogies, elaborate codes of "do's" and "don'ts," and mathematical guidelines were all quite proper, but ordinary Americans, then as now, were unlikely to hold up a tape measure to the flag—instead they measured their own character against it. The number or size of stripes and stars have never mattered as much as the qualities they're said to represent.

According to tradition, George Washington once explained the American flag by saying, "We take the stars from heaven, and the red from our Mother Country, separating it by white stripes, those showing that we have separated from her; and the white stripes shall go down to posterity representing liberty." Other generals and presidents, orators, essayists, even historians have made a host of convincing claims: the white represents purity and hope; the blue stands for justice, fidelity, and loyalty; and the red for valor, courage, and zeal. But no amount of high-flown talk can compare with the way individual Americans have taken the flag into their hearts—and returned it to the general public transformed.

John Philip Sousa gazed at the red, white, and blue in 1897 and created the rousing "Stars and Stripes Forever" march, then George M. Cohan (that "Yankee Doodle Boy" himself) took another look in 1907 and came up with his jaunty hymn of praise, "You're a Grand Old Flag." Impressionist painter Childe Hassam looked at the flag-bedecked streets of New York and captured an era on canvas; realist extraordinaire Norman Rockwell saw how ordinary people treated the flag and turned those vignettes into something far beyond mere illustration.

Yet as much as we thrill to read of the early patriots' escapades and triumphs, as much as we savor the warm glow of nostalgia and unabashed patriotism that songs and paintings from a simpler time evoke in us, the events and images of our own times have the deepest power.

There are men and women living today who remember that the custom of flying the American flag all day and throughout the night over the nation's Capitol first began during World War I; men and women who saw flickering newsreel images of the Stars and Stripes arriving in England to take its place among the flags of the Allies; men and women who cheered among tickertape and waving flags to welcome the "doughboys" home.

Tucked safely away in attic trunks and basement boxes, opened from time to time with great ceremony before the wondering eyes of grandchildren, another generation keeps the relics of World War II: the July 4, 1942, issue of *LIFE* or one of the three hundred other magazines, all of which featured Old Glory unfurled in all its splendor as a rallying point on that first Independence Day when so much of the world lay in the thrall of vicious dictators; the front page of the local newspaper the day it published Joe Rosenthal's Pulitzer Prize-winning photograph of Marines raising the American flag on Iwo Jima on February 23, 1945; the little cloth flags that the children (now parents themselves) waved to the troop trains bustling in and out of the station.

For another generation, the flag is not so much something to touch and feel, but to watch on television. In our mind's eye, we can replay the scenes over and over again: President Dwight D. Eisenhower unfurling the 49-star flag for Alaska in 1959, then the 50-star flag to welcome Hawaii the following year; the first broadcast of the satellite age, when Telstar beamed the flag and the national anthem back down to earth in July 1962; President John F. Kennedy's flag-draped casket being drawn slowly down Pennsylvania Avenue; Neil A. Armstrong's leap onto the lunar surface to plant the Star Spangled Banner on the moon; record-setting 1988 Olympic sprinter Florence Griffith Joyner carrying Old Glory aloft during her victory lap; hostages returning from agonizing captivity bearing tiny American flags in their trembling hands.

We marvel anew each time we reflect on the episodes in which the flag has become indelibly etched in our consciousnesses. Raised in situations our forebears could never have imagined, Old Glory continues to meet new challenges at home and abroad. And wherever the flag goes, there too go the dreams of the American people. Love of country, devotion to duty, national pride—the flag that inspires great acts of public valor, personal sacrifice, and devoted service means something different to each person who sees it. And therein lies its majestic beauty.

The things that the flag stands for were created by the experiences of a great people. Everything that it stands for was written by their lives. The flag is the embodiment, not of sentiment, but of history.

Woodrow Wilson

History

Preceding page: Of the pine trees, beavers, and various other symbols appearing on colonial flags, the rattlesnake emblem was most appealing. American patriots favored this native New World creature as an apt symbol for their cause because they, too, insisted they would not strike unless provoked—and would give fair warning first.

Preceding page: The troops of the Continental Army assembling on New Year's Day 1776 brought along their own individual local flags—but they were pledged to fight *together* under General George Washington and bring honor to a new banner. Combining British crosses with the red and white stripes of the Colonies, hinting that there was still hope for reconciliation, it was known as the Grand Union Flag. **This page:** Did she or didn't she? Historians may quibble over the role Betsy Ross played in the creation of the first American flag, but ever since her grandson told his version of how the Stars and Stripes came into being, artists and storytellers—indeed, the entire American public—have taken Betsy into their hearts as a delightful symbol of creativity and patriotic devotion.

Early flagmakers interpreted the first American flag resolution's specification "thirteen stars . . . representing a new constellation" quite imaginatively. Stars arranged in a circle (above) were popular, while Long Islander John Hulbert (who some historians think deserves at least equal billing with Betsy Ross) placed the stars in a geometric cluster (below). **Opposite page:** Recalling the valor of "The Heroes of '76," a modern reproduction of the Grand Union Flag billows and snaps in the early morning breeze over the battlefields of Yorktown, Virginia, in the Colonial National Historical Park.

Preceding page, above: These three national flags flying peacefully together above a silent cannon recall the often bitter struggles of the Colonial era. The people of Fort Niagara lived under a succession of flags: the French colors, first hoisted in 1726; the British ensign during and after the Revolutionary War; then finally in 1796, the Stars and Stripes. **Below:** Since almost a full year passed between the Declaration of Independence and the first official flag resolution, a lingering question remains: What sort of flag did the patriots carry into battle in the meantime? No one can say for sure, but a modern reproduction featuring 13 stripes and stars is a popular feature of the annual reenactment of General Washington's dramatic crossing of the Delaware River to rout British forces in Trenton, New Jersey. **This page:** Flag experts believe this flag, used at the Battle of Bennington on August 16, 1777, is the oldest Stars and Stripes in existence.

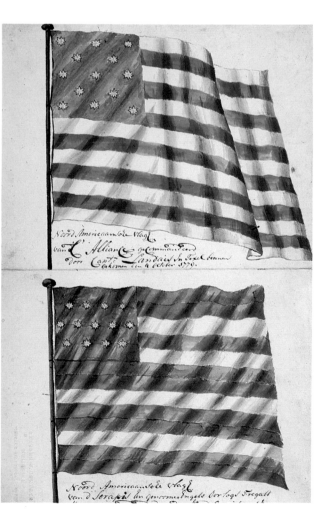

Preceding page, above: Believing American naval Captain John Paul Jones's ship the *Bon Homme Richard* doomed after three hours' battle at close quarters, the captain of the British ship *Serapis* demanded, "Will you surrender?" Jones's reply: "I have not yet begun to fight!" **Below, left:** Jones triumphed, only to watch his ship sink the next morning. In his diary he wrote, "The very last vestige mortal eyes ever saw of the *Bon Homme Richard* was the defiant waving of her unconquered and unstricken flag as she went down. And as I had given them the good old ship for their sepulchre, I now bequeathed to my immortal dead the Flag they had so desperately defended, for their winding sheet." **Right:** The cost in lives was high on land, too, yet the Stars and Stripes eventually prevailed. **This page:** This flag, the original Star-Spangled Banner of 15 stars and 15 stripes (mandated by Congress after the admission of Vermont and Kentucky), waved triumphantly over Fort McHenry in September 1814.

Preceding page: At the beginning of the War of 1812, there were already 18 states; by 1817 Indiana and Mississippi would bring the total to 20. In 1818, "An Act to Establish the Flag of the United States" set forth the pattern still followed today: Thirteen stripes recalling the original colonies and as many stars as there are states. Accordingly, the first flags made the new way featured 20 stars; the banner below may be the only such flag still in existence. **This page, right:** Although Congress set the number of stars, their actual arrangement on the flags carried into battle by soldiers and sailors varied from one "great luminary" to parallel rows, either staggered or aligned. **Below:** When the first settlers headed west on the Oregon Trail in 1842 they carried along their family Bibles, plows, dreams—and 26-star flags. This is one of the most striking designs of that era, the Great Star Flag.

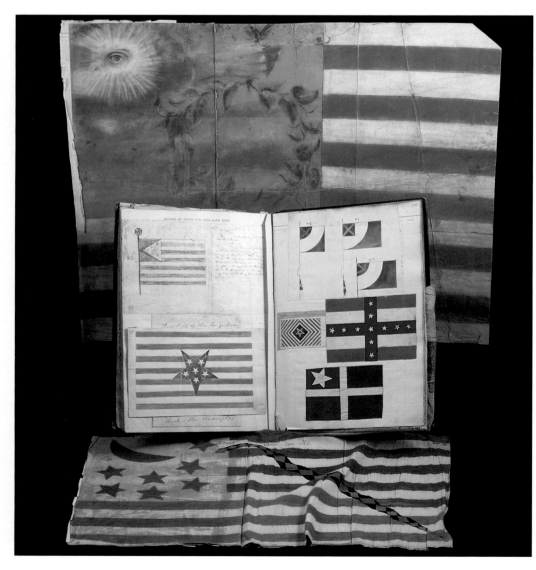

Flag against flag: Kansas' entry into the Union in 1861—as a free state—increased the total of states and stars to 34. But as the Civil War got under way, the fieriest secessionists insisted that *their* stars belonged elsewhere. **Left:** So they held a competition to design a new flag to represent the Confederate States of America.

Below: Of the three official Rebel flags used during the War Between the States, the Battle Flag of the Confederacy provided a vivid, instantly recognizable contrast to the Union forces' Stars and Stripes. **Right:** The Union's battle flags included the "national colors," featuring an eagle with a scroll indicating the unit, and "regimental colors," featuring an appropriate symbol, such as horses for the cavalry. **Bottom:** Spry and feisty at 97, Union stalwart Barbara Frietchie successfully defended her flag against assault by Confederate General Stonewall Jackson's troops.

These pages: Civil War reenacters strive for authenticity in every detail. Union soldiers carry banners complete with gold lettering indicating their regiment or sporting gold fringe, while present-day soldiers of the 9th Texas Infantry, taking a break from camp chores, strike a pose with an early Confederate flag. And in the lull between the fighting, when the Rebels sing "Bonnie Blue Flag," the Union troops will answer:

"Hurrah! hurrah! we bring the Jubilee!
Hurrah! hurrah! the flag that makes you free!"
So we sang the chorus from Atlanta to the sea,
While we were marching through Georgia.

"Marching Through Georgia"
by Henry Clay Work

Preceding page: Though the men of New York City's "Irish Regiment" (also known as "The Fighting 69th") set out in April 1861 with their silken Stars and Stripes at a jaunty angle, Thomas Waterman Wood portrayed their arrival back home in "Return of the Flag" as an occasion for somber reflection. An attempt to return captured Rebel flags in 1887 drew such cries of outrage from the "Bloody Shirts" that President Cleveland revoked his order before it went into effect. It wasn't until 1905 that they were finally returned, without protest. **This page:** A nation mourns: Silent Americans stand watch beneath flags flown at half-staff and buildings draped with black crepe in this contemporary wood engraving of President Lincoln's funeral procession up Broadway in New York City.

Above: In the aftermath of the Civil War, as Americans north and south struggled to re-form their sense of national identity, dramatic improvements in flag-making technology gave Old Glory new prominence. In 1868, an eye-dazzling profusion of flags and bunting transformed the interior of New York's Tammany Hall into a galaxy of red, white, and blue. **Left:** As the nation prepared to celebrate its 100th birthday, even sheet music publishers enlisted the Stars and Stripes to help stir up patriotic feelings.

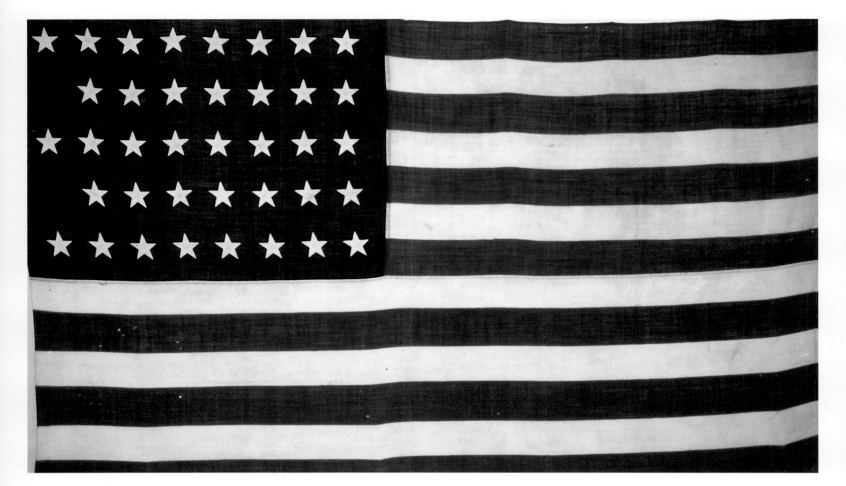

Colorado earned the nickname "The Centennial State" when it was admitted to the Union on August 1, 1876—and provided the nation's flag with its 38th star on July 4, 1877.

Presidential campaign souvenirs, such as this intricate dual-portrait of 1900 Republican candidate William McKinley and his running mate Theodore Roosevelt, offer a great opportunity for "flag waving." Presumably the center shield's 19 stars stand for the new century, since Utah's admission into the Union in 1896 brought the total number of states up to 45. **Opposite page:** In an era that still relied entirely on candidates delivering speeches directly to the public, campaign posters served many purposes. Democratic candidate William Jennings Bryan's flag-bedecked poster features an eye-catching collection of contemporary vignettes, slogans, and patriotic images.

Preceding page: Since 1892, the Pledge of Allegiance to the flag of the United States promised "liberty and justice for all"—and the women of America insisted that meant equal voting rights for both sexes. Whether parading in automobiles or astride horses in Washington D.C., the suffragettes used the flag as a powerful symbol of their cause. **This page:** The 48-star flag, the 25th banner to represent the nation, came into use in 1912 as the suffrage movement gained momentum. For such well-known personalities as playwright Mercedes de Acosta and her sister (above) demonstrating during World War I to the unidentified suffragettes (below) in a Brooklyn parade, a woman's right to vote became a reality when the 19th Amendment was finally approved in 1920.

In 1918, the aptly named American artist James M. Flagg chose the 48-star flag as the background for his immensely popular Marine Corps recruiting poster. **Opposite:** A British tank, displaying Old Glory with equal honor next to her own flag, rumbles along New York's Fifth Avenue as part of the Liberty Loan campaign.

Will you have a part in Victory?

WRITE TO THE
NATIONAL
WAR GARDEN
COMMISSION ~
WASHINGTON, D.C.
for free books on
gardening, canning
& drying.

© 1918 - NATIONAL WAR GARDEN COMMISSION

JAMES MONTGOMERY FLAGG

"Every Garden a Munition Plant"

Charles Lathrop Pack, President

From rural post offices to urban train stations—and everywhere in between—
two other posters by James Montgomery Flagg helped Americans realize the
enormous effort required to win the Great War. Combining a pose reminiscent
of the Romantic artists' ideal of Liberty Leading the People with a face sure to
pass any Hollywood director's screen test, Flagg clothed his victory gardener in
the perfect costume: the American flag. **Opposite page:** A recurring character in
popular culture since the early nineteenth century, Uncle Sam—with his trade-
mark star-studded hat and flag-striped trousers—was already an instantly
recognizable symbol of the United States government when Flagg created this
famous 1918 recruiting poster.

The Eleventh Hour: At 11:00 A.M., November 11, 1918, an armistice between the Allies and Central Powers ended the fighting in the "war to end all wars." In Washington D.C.—and throughout the nation— the American people rushed into the streets in a triumphant paroxysm of emotional release, laughing, crying, shouting—and flag-waving.

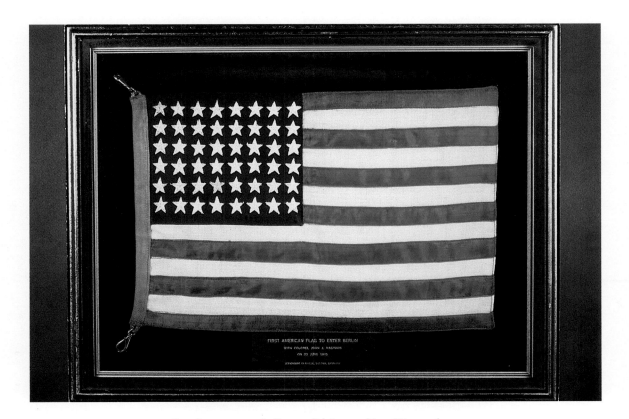

FIRST AMERICAN FLAG TO ENTER BERLIN
WITH COLONEL JOHN J. MAGINNIS
ON 22 JUNE 1945

But the war to end all wars didn't—and just 23 years later American men and women once again left home to fight in foreign lands. Struggling alongside the Allies against ruthless foes and terrible odds, American forces pushed the enemy back, back—until the spring of 1945, when this 48-star banner became the first American flag to enter Berlin.

As Allied forces paraded through the streets after the Liberation of Paris in August 1944, jubilant crowds jammed the sidewalks and balconies to turn *La Ville Lumière,* the City of Lights, into the City of Flags. **Opposite page:** Meanwhile, on the home front, posters, such as this one promoting war bonds, skillfully blended a romantic slogan with patriotic imagery.

To Have and to Hold!

WAR BONDS

OFFICIAL U. S. TREASURY POSTER

Associated with such a multitude of heroic deeds, Old Glory most often inspires the likes of poets, songwriters, and orators. But the simple physical beauty of its stars and stripes is also worthy of consideration. Arranged in a pattern reminiscent of Jasper Johns's celebrated 1958 Pop Art painting *Three Flags*, this eye-popping portrait invites closer inspection. **Opposite page:** Orators, songwriters, and poets keep right on trying to string together enough words to adequately convey what the flag means, but Old Glory's bright stars and broad stripes are best summed up in one word: Freedom.

Arts & Crafts

YOU'RE A GRAND OLD FLAG

GEO. M. COHAN'S SENSATIONAL
PATRIOTIC SONG
ORIGINALLY INTRODUCED IN

GEORGE WASHINGTON JR.

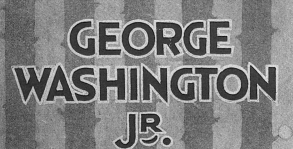

WRITTEN AND
COMPOSED BY

GEO. M. COHAN

MAURICE RICHMOND MUSIC CO. INC.
145 WEST 45TH ST. NEW YORK CITY

Preceding page: The irresistibly toe-tapping rhythms and unabashedly patriotic lyrics of George M. Cohan's song "You're a Grand Old Flag" made it an instant—and persistent—hit ever since its introduction in 1907. **This page:** No one can say for sure if the now-forgotten campaign tune "General Harrison's Log Cabin March" actually helped him win the 1840 election, but the lithograph on the song sheet's cover deserves a vote for "most imaginative use of the flag!"

Here a fanciful quiltmaker combines flags, the Declaration of Independence, popular scenes, and a miscellany of heraldic themes to create a one-of-a-kind, only-in-America original. The flag in the upper right corner is indeed unique—there never was an official 39-star banner. The 38-star flag in use from 1877 through 1890 was replaced in 1891 with a flag of 43 stars. **Opposite page:** This early postcard combines three favorite American symbols: Uncle Sam, Old Glory, and the Statue of Liberty.

Copyright 1907 by Illustrated Postal Card Co.

These pages: Woodcarvers, too, have found inspiration in the Stars and Stripes, creating gems such as a flag-toting fish, a sword-brandishing woman in ship's figure-head style, even a mechanical contraption featuring a bicycle-riding Uncle Sam. Though crafted of solid wood and affixed firmly to the gate, the deceivingly simple Stars and Stripes (opposite, below) manages to evoke the illusion of movement in a gentle breeze.

These pages: Red, white, and blue motifs can add dignity, as in a portrait of Lincoln, or pizzazz, as used on two wooden toys.

"With Freedom's soil beneath our feet
And Freedom's banner streaming o'er us"

Vintage postcards featuring a brave soldier . . .

. . . and a flag-waving young woman recall the unabashed patriotism of
an earlier era.

These pages: From the simple elegance of a real flag sewn onto a quilt to its whimsical use as a "cover" for romance, the American flag has a secure place in our lives—and hearts.

DECORATION DAY

Story of the FLAG.

The red, white, and blue cover of this World War I song sheet captures an important vignette in American history: jubilant dock-side crowds cheering as the doughboys return home in triumph.

Mechanical toys with patriotic
themes continue to intrigue
children of all ages . . .

. . . even when they're as simple
as this cardboard Uncle Sam
with movable arms.

A child's make-believe parade will be complete with the addition of this Uncle Sam doll. **Opposite page:** In a style made famous by Norman Rockwell, artist Randy Berrett depicts Uncle Sam dressing for the annual Independence Day parade surrounded by other favorite All-American symbols. Surely there must be a freshly baked apple pie in that ample picnic basket!

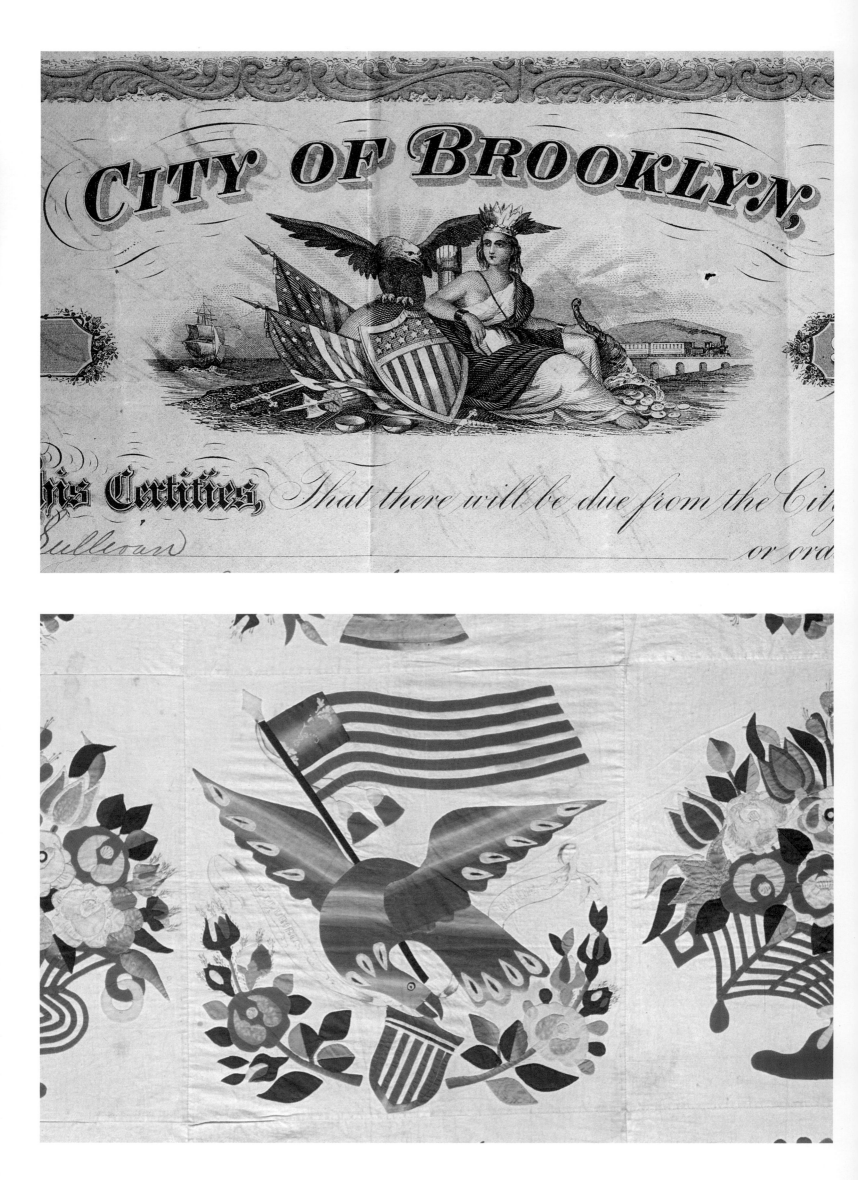

Preceding page, above: The eagle, symbolizing American strength and courage, is a familiar accompaniment to the flag, even when pictured on financial documents. **Below:** In the manner of the eagle depicted on the Great Seal of United States, this quilt-top eagle holds a scroll inscribed with the nation's motto, "E Pluribus Unum"—one from many. **This page:** Immediately popular when introduced as "The Defense of Fort McHenry" in 1814, Francis Scott Key's eloquent paean to the American flag gained popularity as "that Star-Spangled Banner song." During the Civil War Union troops sang it—and Confederates responded with *their* favorite air, "Bonnie Blue Flag."

In tribute to the many ways in which immigrants have enriched American life, fabric artist Barbara Thurman Butler of Marietta, Georgia, entitled this finely detailed work "Of Thee I Sing."

Old Glory and the Statue of Liberty are as inseparably linked with each other in the minds of Americans—and the many foreigners who still dream of living in freedom—as the interlocking squares forming the border on the masterpiece "Lady Liberty" by quilter Lea Hillis of Lee's Summit, Missouri.

The nation's Bicentennial in 1976 inspired all sorts of tributes to the American flag—with plenty of reminders of what life was like in that automobile-less age. In Empire, Michigan, a patriotic farmer painted this delightful "You are here" mural on his barn and included a logger with his team of horses. **Below:** In Grafton, Vermont, an old-fashioned flag has a place of honor next to an advertisement for an equine patent medicine. **Opposite page:** In President Calvin Coolidge's hometown of Plymouth, Vermont, a replica of the Battle of Bennington Stars and Stripes shimmers above an old United States mail coach.

Flags that will never fly: Although two stars short, painted pebbles in Oregon do indeed bring to mind the original Stars and Stripes. **Below:** The stars of a flag mural on the side of a prison in New Orleans must make inmates dream of better days.

A photo montage at Ellis Island melds real-life images of immigrants with the familiar design of our national banner. **Below:** A summertime soft drink display in Charleston, South Carolina, seems to suggest "Things go better with—Old Glory!"

Preceding page, above: Celebrations marking Old Glory's birthday on June 14 typically include patriotic speeches, official proclamations, and recitations of the Pledge of Allegiance. In Gainesville, Florida, the designer of a clamshell flag poses with his unique tribute. **Below:** Either alone or as part of a special commemorative issue, the flag is the most frequently used symbol on American stamps. **This page:** The Stars and Stripes adds the luster of glory to even the simplest building—and reminds passersby of America's magnificent achievement.

Patriotic paint jobs: In Nevada, a convertible (preceding page) sports the ultimate hood ornament, while a Reston, Louisiana mailbox gets "star" treatment. **Following pages, left:** Prison inmates apply the finishing touches to a flag mural featuring a portrait of George Bush. **Right:** Face painted and feather headdress firmly in place, a youngster stands ready to take part in a ceremonial dance at New Mexico's Nambé Pueblo.

Gleaming as if made of rubies and star sapphires, the Citicorp Building's Old Glory
dominates New York City's skyline. **Opposite page:** Inspired by Joe Rosenthal's
February 23, 1945, photograph of the flag-raising on Iwo Jima, the superbly lifelike
figures of this colossal statue stand fast in their moment of victory. But the flag they
raise here is no mere sculptor's illusion—it's real. By presidential proclamation
issued June 12, 1961, the American flag flies here continuously, all day and all night,
a living part of America's proud heritage.

Ceremony & Display

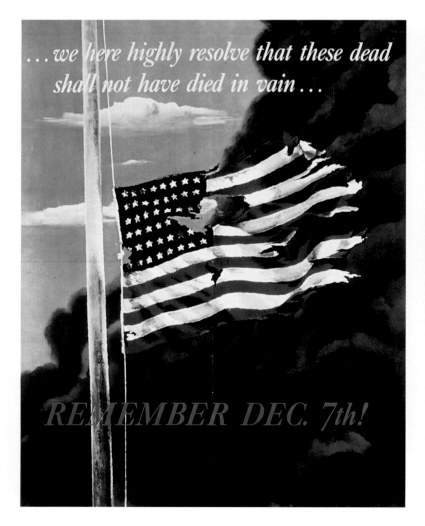

...we here highly resolve that these dead shall not have died in vain...

REMEMBER DEC. 7th!

Preceding page, above: At Oahu, Hawaii's USS *Arizona* Memorial, thousands of visitors daily pause to contemplate the events that propelled the United States into war. Spanning over but not touching the wreckage, the memorial incorporates the *Arizona*'s flagpole, where Old Glory is solemnly raised and lowered each day with traditional Navy honors. **Below:** A phrase from President Lincoln's address at the dedication of the new cemetery at Gettysburg in 1863, featured on a World War II poster (left), and a simple memorial plaque offer us, the living, a poignant reminder of sacrifices made— and the duty that yet remains if we are to carry on their devotion to our country and our flag. **This page:** Early summer sunlight, filtered through the leafy canopy of trees at Arlington Cemetery in Virginia, adds a warming glow to the thousands of flags honoring the final resting place of Americans who've made the ultimate sacrifice.

H WILKENS · EARNEST L WITT · LOUIS J REYNOLDS · PAUL E SCHIE
ZMENDEZ · KENNETH N BLAIR · ROBERT H SANDERS · PEDRO A RODRIGUEZ
OWN Jr · LAURENCE C CAPLAN · JERRY M STONE · DAVID E SWIHART · JAM
HICANTEK · HENRY R CLAUSSEN · HOWARD J ALAIMO · GARY M MARTORELLA · SEVE
FIECHTER · MILTON E FLOWERS · LARRY W BENDER · HAYDN EVANS ·
RD J F HIPPIE · MICHAEL L HORN · HILLIP L BROCKMAN · CALVIN F BUTTERFIELD · JAMES
LD R JENKINS · JAMES C JEWELL Ir · JAMES A CASTLEBERRY · CHARLES L COLEMAN
PH P LOGAN Jr · RONALD L MABE · JOHN A DENNIS · ERIC V DICKSON · JO
MOSES · JOAQUIN NERIS-APONTE · CHARLES H GATEWOOD · WILLIAM G GIFFORD · TH
JAMES R MULLINS · VAN A NORRIS · RUZELL GRAY · LEROY C HALLER · FR
ROBERT K PERRY · JOHN D PETERS · RMAN E HICKS Jr · DOUGLAS M ROGERS · CECIL H H
RK C ROKASKI · JAMES A RUSSELL III · JOSEPH E LAUER · FRANCIS A LAUTNER · THOMA
WILLIAM E SMITH · DANIEL I WEN · SQUIRE N MAYBERRY Jr · O L MIDKIFF · DO
JAMES L BATES · BRADLEY M BO · CHARLES L MORGAN · WAYMAN D MORRIS · JEFF
IGNACIO DURAN · BILLIE H FO · JOSEPH D McNEIL · GLENN N NISHIZAW
ALL C JEREMIAH · CLEM S LOWER · TACIO D QUILALANG Jr · GEORGE M RAMOS · HO
THOMAS W KEMP · JAMES G LATTE · PAUL F SANCHEZ · WILLIE TUCKER Jr · JOH
ONSE J MACCHIONI · MARK E M · OREN F STUDER · DARWIN C STURTZ · JIMMY RA
III · JOHN D PAPE · JOHNNIE E PO · ROBERT J SCHATZMAN · JAMES E WEST Jr
· PAUL BELCHAK Jr · JOHN N BOURNE ·
K W CAMPBELL Jr · JERRY A CAMPBELL · WILLIA
· BILLY E CLARK · JERRY J COLE · MITCH

On a flagpole leaning ever-so-gently against the Vietnam Memorial's wall . . .

. . . resting gently upon a sailor's casket . . .

. . . or reverently draping a Marine's funeral caisson, the American flag calls to mind then-General James A. Garfield's 1868 observation: "For love of country they accepted death, and thus resolved all doubts—and made immortal their patriotism and virtue."

The 13 flags surrounding this statue at the Vietnam War Memorial in Washington D.C.
offer silent proof of the honor and respect due all America's veterans.

In Portland, Oregon, the Color Guard stand ready to lead a Veteran's Day parade. An observance that began on the first anniversary of Armistice Day to honor the soldiers of World War I, November 11 has become a time to honor all America's fighting men and women. **Opposite page, above:** Amid a profusion of flags, and as the plaintive notes of *Taps* sound in the distance, participants in a Veterans Day parade pause for a moment of profound reflection. **Below:** Flag staffs laden with battle streamers, members of each branch of the Armed Services present colors during the Veterans Day ceremonies at the Tomb of the Unknowns in Arlington National Cemetery.

Though best known for their part in public ceremonies on national holidays, members of veterans groups such as the American Legion and the VFW play a vital role all year long, helping insure that each new generation of Americans learns how to honor and respect the flag.

"One flag, one land, one heart, one hand,
One Nation, Evermore!"

Oliver Wendell Holmes

Clockwise: In Colorado Springs, Colorado, thousands gather to wave their flags in support of American troops serving in Operation Desert Storm in 1991. Though no larger than the hands firmly upholding it, this diminutive flag nevertheless speaks louder than the cheers at a Mattoon, Illinois rally for returning Desert Storm troops. At a Fort Stewart, Georgia rally in support of the 24th Infantry, a mother embraces a portrait of her son—and the flag he's pledged to defend.

An American flag waves exuberantly amid New York City's traditional welcoming gesture—a shower of tickertape—during a parade to honor troops returning from Operation Desert Storm.

Reveling in the joys of homecoming, a young soldier adds
his own personal touch to the uniform of the day.

Though her carnation's pungent aroma will eventually fade, this young American is unlikely to forget the day she joined in the flag-waving to welcome home the veterans of Operation Desert Storm.

A giant leap for Old Glory: Soon after Neil Armstrong became the first human to walk on the moon on July 20, 1969, his fellow Apollo 11 astronaut Edwin "Buzz" Aldrin prepared to salute the American flag. Just as the astronauts had to wear special suits to survive in that airless environment, the flag, too, required a bit of American ingenuity: Metal staves had been sewn into it to give it that familiar wind-blown look to the earthlings watching it all on television. **Opposite page:** From the Smithsonian's Arts and Industries Building to the Capitol on Inauguration Day, flags and bunting add a festive air to familiar Washington D.C. landmarks.

Preceding page: The Promise: Like the flag she appears to be saluting in this unusual photograph, the Statue of Liberty recalls old glories—and dreams yet to be fulfilled. **This page, above:** After two years of meticulous restoration work, the Statue of Liberty lifts her torch toward a night sky vibrant with cascading bursts of fireworks—red, white, and blue, of course—during her 100th birthday celebration on July 4, 1986. **Below:** Empty now save for two American flags, the Registry Room on Ellis Island once echoed with the footsteps and voices of masses of newly arrived immigrants, each intent on achieving his or her own vision of the American dream.

Double vision: A bit of photographic magic turns a single row of flags extending from the Chrysler Building on New York's 42nd Street into a double delight.

"The American Eagle—may the shadow of his wings protect every area of our united continent, and the lightning of his eyes flash terror and defeat through the ranks of our enemies!"

Toast, 1818

Manufacturing flags has been a proud tradition at the Annin
Company since 1847—and even though many smaller flags
are constructed entirely with state-of-the-art machinery,
skillful human hands are still required to put the stars together
with the stripes on larger banners.

Summer's amber waves of grain long since harvested, a snow-covered tractor
now serves as a flagpole for Old Glory.

Two American flags beckon from the shady recesses of a sunlight dappled front porch in Cape May, New Jersey.

"There is the National flag. He must be cold, indeed, who can look upon its folds rippling in the breeze without pride of country."

Charles Sumner

A young American offers a salute to an incandescent Old Glory, part of a dazzling display during the Festival of Lights in Ogle Bay Park in Wheeling, West Virginia. **Below:** Under ordinary circumstances, the Flag Code cautions against letting the flag touch the ground—but here in New York's Central Park that's the only way to get this giant ready for display. **Opposite page:** A modern hot air balloon rises into an azure sky bearing an innovative combination of stars and stripes.

From the Salt Lake City Parade in Utah . . .

. . . to the Date Festival Parade in Indio, California, horses and flags are
a crowd-pleasing combination.

Above: Old Glory, Uncle Sam—and the Easter Bunny? Only in America, where whole families often take part in New York City's famed Easter Parade. **Right:** In an Aspen, Colorado parade a diminutive Betsy Ross embraces an impish Uncle Sam.

"Hats off!
Along the street there comes
A blare of bugles, a ruffle of drums,
A flash of color beneath the sky:
Hats off!
The flag is passing by."

Henry Cuyler Bunner's verse offers good advice—
unless, of course, your hat *is* the flag!

Old Glory rippling in the breeze, an orator declaiming in the best high-falutin' style, children playing—an old-fashioned Fourth of July picnic is charmingly captured in every detail of this 1875 engraving entitled *The Day We Celebrate.*

In this 1906 photograph, a young American prepares to celebrate Independence Day in time-honored style with flags and fireworks.

Whether presented by smartly uniformed soldiers . . .

. . . or an aluminum foil-crowned Statue of Liberty, Old Glory is the real star at Fourth of July celebrations.

The Girls of Summer: Three barefoot revelers hold an impromptu parade. **Below:** As long as there are children and wagons, the pioneer spirit will be alive and well in America.

The sun shines bright on Old Glory—and on a young member
of the latest generation to treasure the American flag.

Preceding page: Not all the flags are *in* the parade—in Aspen, Colorado, youngsters on the sidewalk enjoy waving their own banners in a joyous salute. **This page:** As the Space Shuttle lands at Edwards Air Force Base, a boy raises two flags of welcome—and dreams of the day he, too, may be an astronaut.

No mere piece of cloth, Old Glory symbolizes American history, triumphs of physical courage—and bold dreams for a bright future.

United We Stand: Three Colorado friends, faces painted with the familiar red and white stripes of the American flag, join together for a bit of Fourth of July merrymaking.

No Fourth of July celebration is complete until the fireworks display—and this explosion of noise and color over New York's famed skyline provides a breathtaking conclusion to the annual salute to the land of the free and home of the brave. **Opposite page:** At the conclusion of the annual Fourth of July celebrations in Washington D.C., the traditional fireworks extravaganza offers colorful proof of America's continuing devotion to the ideals of liberty—and the glorious flag we so proudly hail.

Index of Photography

TIB indicates The Image Bank.